T0115338

THE PROCESS

FINDING **HOPE** IN **TRAGEDY**

RACHEL RIVERS

WestBow
PRESS®
A DIVISION OF THOMAS NELSON
& ZONDERVAN

WestBow Press books may be ordered through booksellers or by contacting:

WestBow Press
A Division of Thomas Nelson & Zondervan
1663 Liberty Drive
Bloomington, IN 47403
www.westbowpress.com
844-714-3454

ISBN: 978-1-6642-0752-3 (sc)
ISBN: 978-1-6642-0723-3 (e)

Print information available on the last page.

WestBow Press rev. date: 10/20/2020

CHAPTER 1

'The Phone Call'

4:30AM. I WAS JUST ABOUT TO HEAD OUT THE DOOR TO work when the phone rang. At first, I thought it strange to get a call that early in the morning. I almost, never did. However, my first thought was, it was my son, Ray, calling me to wish me a good day, and share with me what he had been working on the night before. You see, we had spoken just hours before I had gone to bed. Ray and I shared a love for music. We had worked on several projects together. Like me, music was an outlet for my son. A way to express ourselves. My son was a producer/song writer. He produced and recorded several songs for me. It was his passion. He put all he had into it. Even made several videos. That night, He told me he had found his hard drive that contained a great bit of his music, videos, pictures, etc. He sounded, really, excited. Said he was going to work on music most of the night.

I thought for sure it was him, calling me that morning to share his latest project. I could not wait to see what he had come up with. He was really, good at what he did. He was very gifted and talented. He had a heart of gold, and just a joy to be around. He loved people and people loved him.

Well, it was not my son calling that morning. It was his friend, calling to tell me that he was at the hospital, and that I needed to get there as soon as possible. She said that the staff was not telling her anything, and that his family needed to get there as soon as possible. I just remember the sound in her voice. She sounded so shaken. I knew I had to get there immediately, so she gave me the address and I told her I was on my way.

All I remember was trying to keep calm. Ray was just getting over the flu and so I assumed that he was probably having some breathing problems, as he had been suffering with COPD. A lung disease that causes reduced air flow. He had made several trips to the ER before to be treated. I was not sure what was going on. All I knew was, I had to get to him. I just remember praying as I scrambled to gather my purse and keys. On the way, I remember calling my co-worker to let her know that I was headed to the hospital, and that I would be late for work. I told her what was going on and asked that she would pray. She agreed and told me to keep her posted. I assured her that I would. Then we hung up the phone. By this time, my stomach was in knots, and things seemed to now be going in slow motion. It seemed as if I could not get to him fast enough. I just prayed to God to give me strength to deal with whatever I was about to encounter. Still dark out, I remember driving over the mountain and trying to keep myself calm. Praying to God that he was alright. Not knowing what to expect. The twenty-minute drive seem like an hour.

After what seemed to an awfully long trip, I finally arrived at the hospital. I notice as I pulled in the parking lot, that there were two policemen standing there at the entrance. They immediately turn their attention towards me. It was quite that morning. Very few people were there. As I headed towards the door, I notice that the officer's eyes were fixed on me, as if there were waiting on me to show up. Now I realize they were.

Now by this time, I am starting to become anxious. As I made my way inside, I notice the receptionists were just staring at me. It made me extremely uncomfortable. I felt at that point that something serious was going on. I needed answers. Before I could inquire information about my son, I saw my son's friend sitting there in the lobby. She seemed to be in a daze. There was also, a lady there with her, that I had never seen before, which later I found out, was her mother. There standing with them was a police officer. He looked distressed. His eyes were red, as if he had been crying. I will never forget the look on his face when he saw me. When I finally made it to them, I notice my son's friend seemed distraught. She looked as if she had been crying. When I walked up to them, she barely noticed me, so I turned to the officer and identified myself as the mother and asked if he knew anything. Hesitantly the officer answered yes and proceeded to take me to the side to talk to me. By this time, we were interrupted by one of the receptionists, who offered us a private area to talk. Now I am starting to get a little irritated. It seemed to be taking too long to tell me what was going on. Nervously I followed the officer into a private room, where he proceeded to tell me what was going on. None-thing could have prepared me for the news that would soon follow. The officer told me that it was an apparent overdose, and that my son was deceased. I lost it! I could not believe what I was hearing. My heart sunk. It was like a bad dream. It was **devastating.** By this time, we were joined by another officer. Trying to process what I had just heard.

The officers started asking me a lot of questions like, what was my son's drug of choice. And who had he been with that night. Then they informed me that, whom ever he was with that night refused to call 911.Still in shock and disbelief, The officers assured me that they were doing all that they could to find out what happened and, they wanted to make sure there was no fowl-play. They assured me that they would get to the bottom of this. Meanwhile, I was trying to process it all. I could not believe what I was hearing. It was like a bad dream. How could this be happening.

I just remember screaming and collapsing on the floor. It was my worst nightmare. It literally knocked the wind out of me. I had to remember to breathe. I remember crying out to God, asking him why. The Officer tried to console me, but I just fell apart. The pain was horrific. I had just spoken to him the night before. How could this be happening. I remember as I lay there on the floor crying uncontrollably, I remember seeing the faces of those that I would have to tell this terrible news. Knowing that it would break their hearts. Thinking of my mother who was just getting over the loss of her husband, my stepdad. Just one month apart. It just seemed unreal. How could this be happening again so soon. Still mourning the death of my stepfather. I could not believe it. At that point I was trying to pull it together. I knew I had to be strong, but It was almost unbearable.

I needed to call someone. At that point I felt so alone. I needed to tell someone, so the first person I could think of was my coworker, So I called her. When she answered the phone, I just screamed, he is gone!!! He died!! That was all I could get out. I had to hand the phone to the officer. He just kept telling me breathe. I was devastated. My whole world was turned upside down. I knew my life would never be the same. After the officer hung up the phone, I then called my husband. Again, I struggled to get the words out of my mouth, and again I handed my phone to the officer. Then finally my sister. They told me they were on their way. After a while, I was able to pull myself up off the floor. I needed to get out of the hospital and get some fresh air. So, I went out to my car. I was numb. I could not believe this was happening.

Shortly after I made it to my car, my sister arrived and came to me. I was so glad to see her. I needed family there with me. She tried to console me, but to no avail. My precious son was gone. There was none-thing that she could say that would take the pain and the shock away. She was heartbroken. All she could do was stand with me like she always had. I am grateful to have her in my life. I just kept trying to wake up from this nightmare. Everything seemed to be going in slow motion. I remember my stomach was in turmoil, I had to find a bathroom. So, we made our way back into the hospital. As I approached the bathroom, there was my husband. When our eyes met, I lost it all over again. His face confirmed that this really was happening, and that it was not a dream. I just fell in his arms, overcome by grief.

By this time, my nerves had gotten the best of me and I had begun feeling sick at my stomach. After pulling myself together, I finally made it to the bathroom. I remember repeating, over, and over again, to myself out loud,' It is well with my soul'.' It is well with my soul'. It seemed to be the only thing I could do, to keep from losing my mind. As I gathered myself and came out of the bathroom, there was my middle son just sitting there with his hands over his face in shock. I immediately ran to him and put my arms around him. We just held one another while my husband looked on, helplessly. I cannot imagine what they were feeling. At some point my youngest son, joined us. My heart broke for them. I prayed that they were able to hold it together. I can honestly say that that was the darkest day of our lives.

About that time a nurse came out and led us all back to the private family room and spoke with us. She told us that she was nurse that worked on my son when he arrived at the hospital, and that he barely had a pulse when he arrived. She offered us her condolences and assured us that she did all that she could to save him. She told us she was getting him ready for us to see him and, she would come to get us in a little while. I was not sure if I would be strong enough to see him. My heart pound at the thought of it.

After a while it was time to go back. I had to prepare myself mentally. I wanted to see him but not like this. I was not sure if my heart could handle it. The nurse told us to be prepared to see the tubes still in place, where they had been doing CPR on him.

As we proceeded back to see him for the first time, my knees buckled. I stopped in my tracks to gather myself. It was the hardest walk of my life. My middle son held me and told me I got you, and we proceeded on back. And there he was. His lifeless body. His struggle was finally over. We stood there, Speechless. No one said a word. I cannot describe the pain seeing my son laying there. He was the stillest I had ever seen him. Still in disbelief, reality finally set in. He was gone. He had become what he rapped about in his songs. He had lost so many of his friends to drug overdoses, and now he had become the next statistic. The very thing that grieved him, now has claimed him. That day my life changed forever. I knew that I would never be the same.

We stayed with him for a little while just trying to come to grips with what had happened. Preparing to live now without him. JESUS!!! After sitting with him awhile, we realized that it was time to go. The nurses and police still had to conduct their investigation. They would have to perform an autopsy to see exactly what claimed his life. The thought of my son having an autopsy sickened me to my core. But I knew that it was something that had to be done. After bringing myself to the fact that he belonged to the hospital now and eventually to the coroner, we said our goodbyes and we went out. The image of seeing him there lifeless has been with me and will probably always be with me. It has changed me forever.

CHAPTER 2

A Message from God

THAT DAY WE WALKED OUT HOSPITAL, WE JUST STOOD around in the parking lot, numb, and in disbelief. It was so hard to bring myself to leave him there. But there was nothing we could do. He was gone. As we were preparing to take the first steps to living without him, a stranger came up to us. A lady. She had been there at the hospital and was on her way to work. If I remember correctly. She said that God told her to turn her car around and come to us. She said he had a message for us. She said that He told her to tell us, that He would be with us through this. It was like a breath of fresh air. For the first time through this ordeal, I felt God's presence. It was comforting. She went on to say that she did not know what was going on and that she did not need to know. Nearly in tears she repeated, God said that he would be with us, then she asked if she could pray for us. And we allowed her to. God was right there with us at the darkest moment of our lives. Through a stranger, and a prayer, it gave us enough strength to take the next steps as we prepared to go our separate ways. After the prayer, we knew that we had to move on from there, we had been there for a while trying to just come to grips with the reality that my son was no longer with us. And so, we did. We all went our separate ways.

God is still in control!

The drive home was surreal. I remember it being a cloudy, misty day. It was like everything was in slow motion. I felt as though I was in a bubble. The world at that point seemed different. I made it home first. As I pulled into the drive- way still in shock, praying that it was just a dream and that I would wake up soon.

I finally made it to my door and as I entered inside. I remember this deafening silence and incredible since of loneliness. Nothing but memories. Questions. Thoughts. Still trying to process everything. Overwhelming sadness, pain, grief. Hard to breathe at times. I could not pray. All I could do was say,' It is well with my soul'. 'It is well with my soul', reassuring myself, that if God allowed it. I had to accept it. I was reminded that the devil cannot do anything lest God allowed it. I still believed that God was in control and that he was with me. It brought a sense of comfort to my heart. I knew I had to trust him, but at the same time, I felt betrayed by God. I did not even know how to approach God, or even what to say. I really believed that God would heal my son on this side. I prayed for him. Others prayed for him. I saw so many testimonies of others being delivered from this disease. That day my enemy, the accuser was there, accusing God of not loving me, not caring. As if he had done this evil thing to my son. That is just like him. He comes to us when we are most vulnerable, and whisper lies. He is the father of lies.

God is good and if he allowed it, then I knew that I had trust that He would bring me through this. Only God knows how many times my son cried out to him to be free. Only God knows the dept of his pain. The desperation of being free of this horrible disease. It was in a lot of his music. I learned later that he was praying for forgiveness as his body was shutting down. He was crying out to God. That brought great comfort to me. I know that God was with him, and that He had never left his side. Then the Lord spoke to me these words, I will not fail you! He reminded me that He too, knows what it is like to lose a son. At that moment I felt the peace of God come over me. The unexplainable peace of God. I remembered that he had never failed me before. I knew that He was with me. His presence was so strong, in that moment. Gods peace surpasses all understanding. It does not come from things or people. Man cannot give it to you, nor can it be taken away. It only comes from GOD!! Shortly after that experience, I began to have all this questions. The first? Why? Why did God allow my son to die? Why didn't God save him? Did I fail him? Was there more that I could have done for him? Guilt and despair.

CHAPTER 3

The Horrors of Addiction

WHEN MY SON ENTERED REHAB FOR THE SECOND TIME, things really looked promising. It was the second attempt to regain his life back. The first time, he did not stay long. It was a struggle for him. He only stayed a couple nights. Later he shared with me that the dope house was just around the corner. The day he decided to leave rehab, in a desperate attempt, I begged him not to go. The staff and I pleaded with him to stay, but because there were no medical staff there, and my sons fear of becoming sick from withdrawals, made him uneasy, It became hard to convince him to stay. It was extremely cold there. At that time, I had little knowledge of what that was like for a heroin addict. Now I know that the pain that comes with withdrawals, takes precedence over everything. That night, indeed, the withdrawals came. Somehow my son was able to call 911. I imagine now he was having severe withdrawals and was crying out for help. The staff was complaining that he had broken the rules there, his first night. One of those rules were, no phone calls. Only

God knows what my baby was going through that night. The next day he had decided to leave. I pleaded with him not to give up so soon. But his mind was made up. It was made clear to my son and I, that the first night would be the worst. The staff advised me that if he go back to the streets, his chances of survival go down dramatically. It terrified me. My son pleaded with me to take him to his grandmothers. After refusing to go back inside, he left walking. He went one way and I went the other. I remember driving off that day looking out the window at my son. Trying to apply tough love, feeling so helpless. My heart was breaking because I could not get through to him. I was feeling the pressure of enabling him, and I knew that ultimately, it was his choice to leave and there was nothing I could do to stop him. So, he went and stayed with my mother for a little while. And then he eventually stayed with me.

After getting into trouble trying to support his habit, He now faced criminal charges. He had never been in trouble before. It was a very scary time. He was possibly facing some serious jail time. That terrified me. He had a court appointed lawyer to represent his case. This lawyer had dealt with many cases like my sons. He recommended a facility outside of our town maybe an hour and a half away. It was a rehab program that he funded for years. He told us he could not guarantee that my son wouldn't do any time, but that the judge was aware of the rehab and that she had worked with many others in the program and would consider working with my son. He said it had a good success rate, but ultimately it was up to my son to complete it. It was the first hope of saving my son. Getting him the help that he so desperately needed. It was a God sent. At first my son was hesitated, but later agreed that it was the best and only option that we had. He started looking forward to going. He was looking forward to getting his life back, so we got the paperwork together and get the ball rolling.

The day we left for rehab; my son was having withdrawals. He seemed very agitated, and angry. I notice his hands were shaking. Never-the-less, He drove us down. I remember praying all the way. He did not want to talk. So, for half the trip, no one spoke. Though he was angry, my heart was so relieved that he was finally going to get help. I had no idea how sick my baby was. No one did. Only him, God, and his fiancé'. He finally turned on the radio to gospel music, which seemed to calm the atmosphere, and we made our way out.

When we got there, I was really impressed with the staff. They were great. They welcomed my son with open arms. They seemed to have a really, good program. It was Christ based, which for me was a plus. I knew not only was this a physical battle, but a spiritual battle as well, and that they believed in prayer. It gave him structure and accountability. It gave him support and hope, A lot of the men there were recovering addicts who had completed the program and became counsellors and mentors however, they did not play there. They took the program serious. They gave you one time to test positive for drugs. That time was the day of your arrival. If you did not follow the rules you were out of there. The staff had given me a number to call and check on my son as often as I would like because He was not allowed to speak with anyone outside of the ranch directly for two weeks. After calling to check on him I learned that he had had a rough night. He had started having withdrawals and had to be taken to the emergency room. Upon admissions, again, we were advised that this would the hardest night entering the program. Much like the first rehab that he entered. The staff assured me that he would be fine. I was glad that at least I knew where he was and that he was in good company and off the streets. I cannot begin to tell you how many nights I stayed up praying and crying out to God to protect and keep him. Every time I heard a siren or heard of a break in or shooting on the news, it scared me. I would literally hold my breath. Like so many others right now. It was like a constant cloud hanging over my head. Knowing at any moment I could get that dreaded call. We both were in the fight of our lives. After sticking it out and enduring the pain of withdrawals, he managed to finally get clean, he gained his weight back. In just two weeks, when were able to come see him, he looked completely different? My son was back. He was so happy. I finally felt like I could breathe again. He had gained favor with the staff, everyone loved him. His good friend was also in the program, and that helped him. He got a chance to work in exchange for his room and board. He got a job picking up donations. Later he would graduate to driving the truck. He was doing well. I still have the first letter he wrote to me. He was so thankful to God that he was finally sober. Talked about how much clearer things were now that he was sober. He asked about his daughter, whom he loved dearly. And his brothers. He really wanted to see them. Things looked good. I also was thankful. I missed him, but I knew that he needed to get away from the environment that he was in. That he needed structure, accountability. Strong Godly men that would pray for him and mentor him.

My mother and I would come up on Sundays to go to church with him. That was part of the program and we love it.

Church and bible study every week. My mother was my rock. Always ready to ride. My son was like a son to her. His face would light up when he would see us. It was great! Here we were, all in church, worshipping God together. It was powerful. I thank God that we had that experience. It was beautiful.

People would come and tell their testimonies. Some of which had graduated the program and did well. Then there were the sad stories of those who had to come back and reenter the program, and then there were those who did not make it. Their stories were heartbreaking. I knew in my heart that if my son did not stick with the program, that could become his reality. I prayed for him every day. I always had hope. That year we went up to spend Thanksgiving with him and brought a huge feast with us. He quickly invited some of the resident to come and grab a plate. He had a heart of giving. Then Christmas rolled around, and they were having a Christmas program and the residence got an opportunity to showcase their talent. So, Ray decided to do one of his songs. It was awesome. He told me it was the first time in a long time he had performed sober. He was nervous about it at first, but he pulled it off. I was so proud of him. The residence and staff loved him. However, he shared with me that he was having some issues with one of the residences there and had expressed to me that he was thinking of leaving. It was really bothering him. I tried to encourage him to stick it out. And after a while. My son made the decision to leave. I would later get a phone call from his attorney that he had left the program. I remember my heart dropped. I had no idea where he was. It threw me into a panic. After many attempts to contact him. Finally, I was able to get through to him. He told me he had planned on going to a half- way house. He managed to get into a twelve- step program after going to classes with a friend. He expressed to me that he had an opportunity to reconnected with his music partner, and that they had a big project coming up. He wanted to get back home and finish pursuing his music career. He did good for a while. He went to his meetings faithfully. And finished. He even made a music video. He was on top of the world. He was sober and ready to get back to his music.

But it was not long before what he had left, found him again. This time he kept it hidden from me. I never got a chance to help him. Now when I think about it, he hinted to me that he was possibly struggling again. Maybe I did not want to believe it. Now I deeply regret never asking him how he was doing. I would have gone through the whole process of getting him back in the program. Whatever it took. Now it is too late.

I could not understand why God allowed him to leave us. Why did God not save him? He wanted to be free. When I think about it now, maybe that is why. I remember how happy he was when he went to rehab and got clean. He wrote me and told me how he was grateful to God to be sober. He was looking forward to the future. His dream was to make it big and take care of his family. He had a heart of gold. The devil knew that and hated him for that. Often, he would show up through people. My son expressed to me that it was hard to focus on getting better. People were jealous of him because not only was he extremely handsome, but he had the personality to match. Most people adored him. My son would always wear a smile, even when he was hurting. He hid it well. The drugs numbed the pain. That is what they do for a season.

CHAPTER 4

'My Faith Was Shaken'

I REMEMBER SITTING THERE ALONE IN MY GARAGE THAT day after leaving the hospital desperately needing to hear from God. I was feeling so much guilt. Could I have done more to save my son. I was feeling like I failed him. I knew I needed to pray, but I did not know what to say to God. After all, He allowed it! I could not even watch Christian programming. I had called a few of them for prayer, and believed that he would pull through, and I still lost him. I felt like I had failed him. And now Here I sit all alone in this indescribable pain. Shock, disbelief. How could God allow this? Then in my spirit I felt like God was saying," I will not fail you". In a still small voice, the Lord spoke to me. I cried like a baby. I felt his presence like I had never felt before. God was more real to me then, than I had ever experience before. Ever!!!!

The very next day I woke up, still hoping that it was all a dream. That pain was right there waiting for me to awake. God in his graciousness, allowed me to sleep sound throughout the night, just like the night of my son's passing.

There were times that God warned me of dangers that my son was in through dreams. I would wake up from nightmares of his death, then I would pray. Later my son shared with me how he almost died from an overdose. Just two years before his death, I had several dreams that he had died from an overdose. I woke up crying and praying to God. At one time I shared the dream with him. I pleaded with him after he got clean to not go back to it. I realize now that it is not that simple. I wondered why God did not warn me this time. I had so many questions.

That night after talking to my son for the last time. I went to sleep feeling good. It was so good talking to my son that night. He sounded happy. Though in the back of my mind he sounded too, happy. I questioned myself that he might be high, but I never brought it up. I guess I did not want to believe it. Now I wish I had said something. Would it had made a difference? I do not know. I believe he wanted to reach out to me, but the shame and the stigma of being an addict kept him in the dark. He did not want to worry me.

I think about the last time I saw my son alive. He came up to my job. He told me that he had the flu and that he needed money, so that he could go to a walk-in clinic. I now wonder was it for the clinic or was it for his next fix. All I know is he was so sick that day. I prayed for him and I held him close to me. When I got ready to go back inside, he held me, and he did not want to let me go. I believe he was screaming for help, that his heart was breaking. trying to tell me then that he had had a relapse. Why didn't he tell me? Why didn't I know? I am so sorry that I did not know.

After my son had gotten clean for a few months, he shared with me how he would ask me for money, and would lie to me about the things he needed the money for, only to buy drugs. He said he would get the money from me and he would cry. He hated it. I cannot imagine what he was going through.

My son was addicted to heroin. His addiction started with pain pills, prescribed by his doctor. Like so many thousands today. By the time I found out he had been battling addiction, he was in deep. He had been battling it for years. I had no idea. I had no knowledge of this disease. I did not know just how serious it was and how it works. I know now that it can permanently alter a person's brain. It rewires the brain in such a way that normal pleasure is non- existent. I know that the pain of withdrawal is extreme and intense. I witness my son going through withdrawals. He was shaking violently. It was nearly unbearable to watch, and I felt helpless. I remember one day I drove him to the ER as he was having withdrawals. Little was done for him. He had no insurance, he could not hold a job because of this addiction. I remember feeling so helpless. He told me he had to use before he could even go out anywhere and when the drug would start to wear off, to escape the pain, the chasing for the drug would begin. He shared with me that even when he got the hit, in the back of his mind was, that it would wear off. It was a vicious cycle that seemed to never end. He told me that it was hard to enjoy life. Only God knows want my son was going through, maybe that's why God called him home. I took comfort in the fact that

My son had given his life to The Lord at an early age. I believe he is in heaven now. What Christ did for us on the cross. How he died for the sins of the world. How he makes all things new, gave me the grace to bear it. The gospel really came alive in my life at the passing of my son. Now I understood what it really means to be save.

CHAPTER 5

Conversations with God

I REMEMBER DAYS OF JUST FEELING SO EMPTY. AFTER I WAS finally able to make it back to work. By the grace of God, I was able to make it through my days, but most days, for a while I would cry all the way home. Life looked and felt different now. It was not the same anymore. One minute my son was so full of life, and now he wasn`t. My son and I were worlds apart. I could not talk to him anymore. The thought of never hearing his voice again. Never receiving a text from him was heart breaking. A piece of me died with him. I could not eat. It was hard for me to pray. I did not know what to do with myself. All I had now was memories. Regrets. I remember asking God, what do I do with this pain.

I was totally emptied out. Broken. My life was turned upside down. My world has been shattered. I needed to just keep breathing. It hurt well beyond words. I had to remember to keep breathing. When one suffers from addiction, the whole family suffers.

After my son's death, I remember thinking, ok God, you have got my attention. Here I am Lord. What do I do next? I was totally depending on God from one breath to another. One moment of every hour, of every day. to the next. I had to learn to trust God, and to trust that He was still in control. I had to remember that despite it all, He is still good. Though I lost a son, I still had two. Sometimes we must look back and remember all the things that God has given us, and all the good things done. All the prayers that were granted. Sometimes He does not always give us what we ask for, but He always gives us what we need.

Someone very dear to me said something so profound to me. She said, "God sees far more than we can see". That is true. He sees far down the road. He knows what is around the corner. He sees all things. He is all knowing. The question is will we still trust Him when things go wrong? When we cannot understand why, will we turn from him, or will we run to Him?

I made the choice to run to Him. To worship Him through the pain. I chose to make Him bigger than my problems. Quite frankly, He is. God is greater than anything that we could ever go through. He can get us through anything that we could ever face if we turn to Him. After I made that decision in my heart to turn to God, supernaturally I felt the strength and, peace and power of God over-shadow me. He was my source and strength and was the only way I would get through this.

Till this very day, worship has been my weapon. I had a dream very on early in my life. In the dream, I was in a room with extremely limited light. I felt like the room was closing in on. I was surrounded by evil beings. Perhaps these beings represent demons. As they were closing in on me, I remember lifting my hands and just worshipping God right there in the amidst the darkness. Then the demons began fleeing from my presence. They ran out several different ways. Powerful. God inhabited my space and the enemy had to flee.

Praise and worship are valuable weapons that God gave His people for the battle. It fights off depression and confusion. It welcomes God into any situation. We place God back on the throne where He should be. It says to the enemy that God is greater than anything that comes our way. We allow God to fight for us. None-thing and no-one can stand against Him. Apart from God, we can do none-thing but with God all things are possible. Depression and fear come from the enemy. God has not given us a spirit of fear, but of love. And of power, and a sound mind. **2Tim 1;7 KJV**

CHAPTER 6

'My Spiritual Eyes Were Wide Open'

AFTER THE DEATH OF MY SON, MY SPIRITUAL EYES WERE wide open. Life as I had known it was changed. People looked different to me. I saw them as walking miracles. That is what we are. Miracles. After seeing my son who had so much life so much energy one day, and seeing him the next day, lifeless. It was an eye opener. The very breath that we breathe belongs to God. Things that I stressed about before, did not matter at all. I wanted to forgive people immediately. I wanted to love harder. Giving myself away seemed to be the one thing that helped me forget about my pain for the moment. I began getting glimpses of God's character. I began seeing things in a different light. Through the eyes of God. Giving myself away and making myself available was my first steps to the healing process. I am reminded of a time, just weeks before my son's death, I was on my way to work. I was crying out to God on my son's behalf.

Praying and asking God to heal him. And in a still small voice, I heard in my spirit, 'Forgive him.' I was not sure why I was hearing this, but I knew it must have been from God. God sees far better than we can. And so, I told the Lord, 'I forgive him.' It was not long after that that the unthinkable happened.

After my son's death I remember trying to make sense of it. Trying to find purpose for my life. Believing that something good must come out of it. I started trying to keep busy. Trying to connect with others who had similar losses. I went to support meetings; I even took part in a walk in my town to end drug abuse. Hundreds attended. I was trying to find purpose in my pain. Somehow, I found a sense of comfort knowing that I was not the only one that had lost a child to an overdose. According to a study I researched, in 2018, the year my son died, 67,367 people died of a drug overdose. It was also reported that 128 people die a day. Sons and daughters, mothers, fathers. Brothers, sisters. Wives, husbands. Aunts and uncles. Cousins and friends. Even grandparents. They are not just statistics. They are people who had lives, families, dreams. The loss is great. Two years later, I still miss him dearly. Not a day has gone by, that I do not think of him. Every birthday. Every holiday. Though the pain has gotten better, it still hurts. Some days, it is like it just happened. Some days it is still hard to believe that he is gone. But God has given me the grace to keep going. I know that he would have wanted it that way. That was just like him. He had a heart of gold.

'Purpose in Pain'

For a while I found myself trying to understand why God aloud my son to be overtaken by this addiction. I understand now that God can- not be understood, He can only be revealed. I realize that God's ways are perfect. He is a perfect God and He is all knowing. Though I may never understand fully why I suffered this great tragedy, I know that I am not alone in it. Countless stories of overdoses and near-death experiences, because of overdose, occur, every day. Thousands of lives lost. Thousands of families, lives shattered by addiction. Thousands of people scrambling, trying to pull their lives back together. Every story different, but not less painful. Children who have lost a brother, or sister. A mother, or father. A son or daughter. For me? I had to trust that God would be with me in it and bring me through it.

I had to make a choice that either I would let this tragedy make me bitter or make me better. I chose better. After all, I had witnessed so many miracles in my life before. I had seen people recover from cancer miraculously. I had seen people survive from heart attacks, and stabbings. Gunshot wombs. I had witnessed the power of prayer. I have seen God's power at work in so many others and even in my own life, time and time again. I knew that there was nothing that God could not do. And though my circumstances had changed, that He had not changed. I knew that He was still God and that He was still on the throne. He remined me that He would never fail me and that I could trust my pain in His hands. After the visits, and the phone calls stopped. I found myself alone. Life continued to go on and no amount of pain could stop that. How we process the pain, however, is another matter. I am grateful for the outpouring of love and support from my family and friends. Co-workers. I am grateful for those who stepped up and helped me put together my son's funeral, and homegoing service. I am thankful for every text and or message I received from those who too had lost a child and could understand that kind of pain. I valued their stories greatly because we could relate on another level. Seeing how they had survived it and was able to keep going, had given me strength to believe that I too would get through it as well. And I did. I believe that these acts of kindness and the very people that God had surrounded me with were the very hands of God. I was suffering a broken heart, like so many today. I also knew that healing for me would take time.

I can honestly say that it has made me stronger. My faith has increased. It was those times when it was just God and me. It was in those times that God began revealing himself in ways that I had never seen before. Maybe it was because of the emptiness I felt at that time, and how desperately I needed to hear His voice. He began to give me His vision and His heart. He allowed me to see people and things, through his eyes. The miracle of life. He reminded me of the love that He has for my son, and that was far greater than I could have ever loved him. He reminded me that my son belonged to him. That He is the Father that my son always longed for. I began to have a heart for those who are struggling with addiction. I would see my son in them. Compassion would fill my heart. Even today.

Writing this book has been very painful, and yet, therapeutic. Reliving the events of that day, those painful memories of losing my son. For a while, I did not want to be alone with my thoughts. I slept a lot. Worked long hours. Anything to try and keep my mind preoccupied. But in the back of my mind, it never seems to go away. Though God gave me the strength to go to work and still be productive, must days thoughts, and memories of my son would consume me. This went on for months. At times I thought I was losing my mind. I can say now that it will get easier.

I think of my mother. Her and my son were close. She told me that he was like a son to her. She lost her husband, my stepdad to a massive heart attack, after battling with diabetes. After losing both his legs to the disease, his hearing and sight, and several shots of insulin to control the disease, along with countless amounts of medication. He finally succumbed to this unforgiving disease. He was also close to my son. My son always wanted to be around them. He spent a lot of time with them. They loved having him around. They loved their grandchildren, and their grandchildren adored them.

The death of my son's grandfather was a devastating blow. Not just to my son, but to all of us. He has always been in our lives. The loss was huge. My son took it extremely hard. He spent a lot of time with my mother, weeks before his death. He told me they had become closer He felt comfortable being there with her because she was never judging or critical. I think we all should be that way.

After my stepfather's death, my son was not the same. He seemed to be in a daze right after it happened, up until the of night of his death. He had paid my mother a visit that night. She later told me that he wanted to share something with her, but he was afraid that she would tell me. Only God knows what that was. My mother told me that he seemed sick that night. I cannot imagine what he was going through that night. He told her that the wrong company was showing up, and that he was there to get away. It breaks my heart to think that he did not come to me. Looking back, I remember weeks before my son's death, he began reaching out to me about past differences and misunderstandings he had had with my husband. He told me that my husband was good for me. That he understood that he was out of line at times. It was like he was trying to make things right. I remember thinking, 'where was this coming from'? At one point in the conversation, He got choked up. I believe again he was trying to reach out to me. I believe he knew that he was in danger. I believe he was preparing himself for the journey. The memories of my mother, seeing him one last time the night of his death, must have played in her mind over, and over again. She told me she thought of him often and would have dreams of him. She was now, grieving the death of her husband, and her grandson. She was now alone. I can't imagine the pain she was suffering.

CHAPTER 7

The Journey Home

My mother had talked about moving back home after my stepfathers passing. She wanted my son to come and stay with her. She loved him being there with her. He cooked for her. He made her laugh. They were so close. I loved to watch them interact. I saw myself in them. The pain of losing them so sudden, so close together, was nearly unbearable, **BUT GOD!!** He really is a sustainer. I remember someone said to me after the deaths of my son and my mother. 'They still live through me'. Powerful. They were encouragers. They loved to laugh. They brightened and touched the lives of those they met. They always believed the best in people, despite their struggles. They always had hope. They were believers. I learned so much from them and now my mission is to live in a way that would honor them, as well as honor God. Today I am determined to survive and continue to live. That is how we can honor our loved ones that have gone on home. **Keep living!** My mother was strong in the faith. She loved the Lord. She was my rock after my son died.

We had so many conversations about heaven. We talked about my son and my stepfather all the time when we were together. But mostly we talked about our God. And how good He had been to us. We rejoiced over the truth that because of the cross and because Jesus died for us that we would see them again in heaven. John3;16 KJV says," For God so loved the world that He gave His only begotten son, that whosoever believed in His shall not perish, but have everlasting life." My mother and I rejoiced in the fact that if God said it, then we believed it, and that settled it. It was the hope we needed to keep going.

We began spending even more time together. Every weekend that I was off, we were together. We often had church driving down the road. She was an amazingly strong woman. She had the gift of charity. Always saw the good in everyone. Patient and kind.

We talked about everything. She was my best friend. Gentle and soft spoken. Yet strong and enduring. She suffered many great losses. She was an overcomer. She loved everybody. Opened her home to nearly everybody that need a place to lay their head. She was a nurturer.

Nearly a year after my son passed, my mom also went home to be with the Lord.

She had a massive heart attack. She had been battling heart disease for a while.

She had become very thin and frail. Life had really taken a toll on her. She endured so much. The weekend before her passing, we spent most of the day together shopping. It was like a typical Saturday. It was our special time together.

Towards the end of our trip, she seemed tired, so I took her home. I did not think much of it. She seemed fine that day. That Saturday I kissed my mother good-bye, and told her that I love her and, that I would see her soon, and that following Tuesday she was gone. She finally made home to the place she longed for. The place we had talked about that very weekend. That placed that lit her face up every-time we talked about it. That place that gave her great joy. I am most grateful for those memories today. Thank God for those memories, and the opportunity to experience that.

When I lost my mother, I grieved in a different way. It was not like I had expected. There was this overwhelming sense of peace that cannot be explained. Yes, the pain of separation was, and is today, still real. I miss her like you would not believe. I believe God had prepared me for the passing of my mother through the passing of my son. I started thinking of heaven more after my sons passing. And now I believed that they were together again, in heaven. I cannot imagine what the reunion was like. My mother was an amazing woman. She taught me how to love. Even when it hurt. She was humble and meek. Soft spoken yet strong. I believe the world needs more people like her. She was the strongest woman I know. Beautiful inside and out. She endured much. She remained a soldier till the end. She was selfless and more than often, put others before herself. She did not have much but what she had she gave. Like the woman in the bible that gave all she had. Jesus declared her blessed. I truly saw Christ in her. She loved him And He loved through her. She saw me through so much. The good times and the bad times. At times we would get together and praise our way through. I have so many memories of her and I driving down the road having church. I am honored and thankful to God to have had her in my life. So many beautiful memories that I can hold on to that for the rest of my life.

I cannot imagine all the times she prayed for us. Or many times she cried for us and pleaded to God on our behalf. She was an amazing woman. She loved her kids and would do anything for us. Just before my mother died, the family suffered another great loss. My great-niece died suddenly from sudden infant death, or 'SIDS' just weeks old. I never even got to meet her. She was beautiful. Pure. It was an incredibly sad time for my family. My heart broke for her mother. And for my brother and his family. We had gone to so many funerals that year. Before we could get over one heartbreak, our hearts would be broken again. We could not understand why. All we could do was look to God and each other for strength. And with Gods help, we got through it together, and continue to push through the healing process. My mother is deeply missed. She was like the glue that held us together. She was utterly amazing. I will miss her dearly. I think of all that I wanted to give her while she resided here on earth, and now, she has it all. She has a mansion in heaven, not built with human hands. She is now reunited with her husband. Her mother. Her father. Her sisters. Her brother. Her grandson. Her great-grand-daughter. Her daughter. Aunts and uncles. Friends and acquaintances. Her assignment there is probably to oversee the nursery. She loved children. But most importantly, she expressed to me many times before that she would finally get to see the face of her Savior, Jesus Christ. The one that made this reunion possible.

I believe if she could say anything to us today it would be what she has said all along. Get to know Him so that you can join us when your time comes.

I take great joy in knowing that something so painful can be precious to God. I know that my mother and my son, and many of my loved ones are now with the Lord. So great a place, absent from suffering and pain. Though we can never understand God's ways, we can always trust them. Though we cannot see Him with our physical eyes, He is always with us. Truth is, He has always been with us. In the darkest times. As our world faces one of the worst attacks of evil, with this disease. I still see God. He is with us. He is the hands of our healthcare workers. Those that risk their lives on the frontline everyday attending to those sick and dying.

Those who minister his love in deeds. It has been a reminder how precious and short life is. The process of healing for me has been a slow one. There is not a day that goes by that I do not think of them. Somedays it feels as if it just happened. But through it all, I have learned to trust that God would be with me and my family through it. Till the end. So far, He has been faithful. And though this would never have been the book I would have written for my life, just maybe if it gives someone encouragement that they will survive the painful process of grief. That you will smile again. That not only will you survive, but if you turn to God and trust Him with your pain, He will heal you and make you stronger than you have ever been. He will never leave you alone. What I have learned. Love like it is your last day. Forgive always. And if possible, as quick as possible. The sooner you forgive, the sooner the healing process can begin. Always see the good in everyone. People are miracles of God. Created in His image. This life is temporary. God has a far greater plan for us. That plan is to bring us home to be with him. Christ Jesus died for every living soul to make that possible. All we must do is believe and allow Him to come into our hearts. He has already paid the price. You may never have that chance again. I pray that this book will inspire others to turn to God. This book is dedicated to my family, and all those who have suffered great loss. Or maybe are going through one of the darkest times of your life. John16:33 KJV "These things I have spoken unto you, that in me ye might have peace. In the world ye shall have tribulations: but be of good cheer; I have overcome the world.

THE END!

ABOUT THE AUTHOR

RACHEL RIVERS IS A FIRST TIME AUTHOR AND MOTHER OF three. Born and raised in Hunstville Alabama with a love to write. Born-again believer of Jesus Christ.

Printed in the United States
By Bookmasters